Wildlife in the City

True, most animals are found in the wild, sparsely inhabited areas of the United States. However some professional types of animals can be found in our major cities. Actually, entire teams of them can be found. Do you know what city to associate with each of the following teams?

Colts _____

Sharks _____

Cardinals _____

Tigers _____

Marlins _____

Rams _____

Bulls _____

Seahawks _____

Broncos _____

Dolphins _____

Whalers _____

Falcons _____

Orioles _____

Panthers _____

Bengals _____

Eagles _____

Timberwolves _____

Cubs _____

Bears _____

Hornets _____

Ravens _____

What other animals would be good names for mascots of professional sports teams?

_____

_____

_____

_____

_____

Why is no professional team nicknamed the Kittens or the Puppies?

_____

_____

_____

_____

A "T" for Thousands

Every state has a flag, bird, motto, flower, animal and nickname. Congress just passed a law that every state must have an official T-shirt to sell to tourists. Here is your chance to become famous. Design the official T-shirt for your state. You can hold this sheet to a window and draw the back side so you can design both sides. The shirt should have a slogan as well as a design.

The Good, the Bad, and the Ugly

THIS IS MY COUNTRY. LAND THAT I LOVE FOR BETTER OR FOR WORSE

Compare and contrast. What would people from various foreign countries find to be the most or least in the United States?

most attractive _____

unattractive _____

new _____

old _____

humorous _____

scary_____

ugly_____

tiny _____

boring_____

weird _____

embarrassing_____

common _____

polluted _____

useful _____

unpleasant _____

beautiful _____

large _____

exciting _____

ordinary _____

proud _____

spectacular _____

wasteful _____

useless _____

pleasant _____

Now add some of your own examples based on the above formula.

_____ _____

_____ _____

_____ _____

_____ _____

_____ _____

_____ _____

_____ _____

_____ _____

Cities vs Towns

Name a couple of cities in your state. _____ and _____
.

Name three of the largest cities in the United States. _____
_____

Name several towns in your state. _____
_____

1. What is the difference between a city and a town? _____
_____
_____
_____

2. What are some things you can find in a city but cannot find in a town? _____
_____
_____
_____

3. What can you find in a town that you can't find in a city? _____
_____
_____
_____

4. Why do some towns become cities and some do not? _____
_____
_____
_____

5. Can a city become a town? How? Why? _____
_____

6. During a disaster (tornado, earthquake, power failure) would you rather be in a city
or in a town? (Circle one.) Why?
_____
_____
_____

4

Cities vs Towns

Name a couple of cities in your state. _____ and _____
.

Name three of the largest cities in the United States. _____
_____

Name several towns in your state. _____
_____

1. What is the difference between a city and a town? _____
_____
_____
_____

2. What are some things you can find in a city but cannot find in a town? _____
_____
_____
_____

3. What can you find in a town that you can't find in a city? _____
_____
_____
_____

4. Why do some towns become cities and some do not? _____
_____
_____
_____

5. Can a city become a town? How? Why? _____
_____

6. During a disaster (tornado, earthquake, power failure) would you rather be in a city or in a town? (Circle one.) Why?
_____
_____
_____

On the Move

For the past twenty-five years or so Americans have been on the move. California, Texas, Nevada, and other "sunbelt states" have experienced population growth. There has been a significant shift of people from rural to urban areas. Many suburban areas have experienced significant growth. Much of this population shift has been caused by the economy and climate. People want to move where the weather is more hospitable or they need to move where there is employment.

How can we get people to move to the wide open spaces? What could entice people to move to Wyoming, the Dakotas, or Alaska? Create a list of ways these more rural states could entice people to live there. Brainstorm!

_____

_____

_____

_____

_____

_____

_____

_____

Job Possibilities: _____

_____

_____

_____

_____

Recreation/Leisure Time Possibilities: _____

_____

_____

_____

Living Advantages: _There is less pollution._

_____

_____

_____

_____

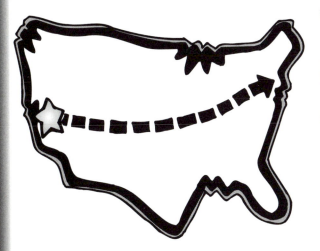

What's Between New York and California?

If you were asked, "What's between your ears?" included in your response would be "My nose, tissue, veins, my eyes, two corneas, some thinking, cartilage, flesh, tubes, bone, and hair." The list could continue on and on.

Answer the following question a variety of different ways.

What's Between New York and California?

Nevada, Pennsylvania and seven other states.

_____
_____
_____
_____
_____

Mountains, deserts, farms, rolling hills, plains.

_____
_____
_____
_____

About four days of driving or a six-hour flight.

_____
_____
_____
_____

Not Everyone Lives in a House

True, millions of people live in a house. At least in small town U.S.A., most people live in a house. However, millions of people live in something other than a house. People in New York City live in condos, apartments and lofts. Abraham Lincoln lived in a log cabin. Complete the chart below according to the examples. Each type of dwelling listed must be different.

Type of Dwelling	Location	Details
house	Hope, Arkansas	Bill Clinton lived there.
igloo	500 miles north of Anchorage, Alaska	no air-conditioning needed
travel trailer	Quartzite, Arizona	winter only – Bill and Mary Murphy – retirees

Does Monkey's Eyebrow, KY Really Exist?

It would not take a mental genius to determine how Big Springs, TX got its name. The same is true for Big Sky, MT and Round Lake, IL. Some communities (Lincoln, NE) are named after a famous person. Others are named by their discoverer or first settler. Places like Lihue, HI and Shaktoolik, AK are named from words in the native language of that area. However, the names of some communities leave much to the imagination. Put on your thinking cap and create an explanation for the origin of the names given to the following cities, towns and wide spots in the road.

What Cheer, IA (population 762) _____

_____

Santa Claus, IN (927) _____

_____

Okay, OK (526) _____

_____

Baraboo, WI (9,203) _____

_____

Truth or Consequences, NM (6,221) _____

_____

Zap, ND (287) _____

_____

Kissimmee, FL (30,050) _____

_____

Soddy Daisy, TN (8,240) _____

_____

Cowpens, SC (2,176) _____

_____

Choose one of the above communities and write a letter to the Chamber of Commerce or mayor of the community and seek information so you can compare your version of how the community actually got its name. Do a little research. Use an atlas and see if you can discover additional unique names of communities.

5 X 5 Equals 25

Five times five equals twenty-five and that is a perfect score.
A perfect score is what you should try to get in this geography
game. There are five letters of the alphabet and five
categories. You should try to fill in each square of the grid with
an appropriate answer.

For example you need to think of a state that begins with the letter *M*. Lucky you! There
are many possibilities: Mississippi, Missouri or Michigan. Think of one more and write it in
the blank square. Next you need to think of a capital city that begins with the letter *M*.
There are three. Write one in the blank square.

Then you are asked to think of a river, geographic feature (marsh, mountain), and a tourist
attraction that begins with the letter *M*. Sounds pretty easy. Just give it a try.

If you enjoy this game, create a similar one for a friend or enemy to try.

	State	Capital	River	Geographic Feature	Tourist Attraction
M				mountains	
S					
D					
P					
C					

Attributes

Attributes are characteristics. Characteristics are traits. Think about yourself for a minute. What are your attributes? Are you tall, young, blonde, friendly, intelligent? A baby kitten is soft. A California redwood tree is gigantic. Rhode Island is small when compared to Alaska. What are some attributes of the United States. Write one attribute of the United States in each of the states. Along the east coast you may need to use arrows.

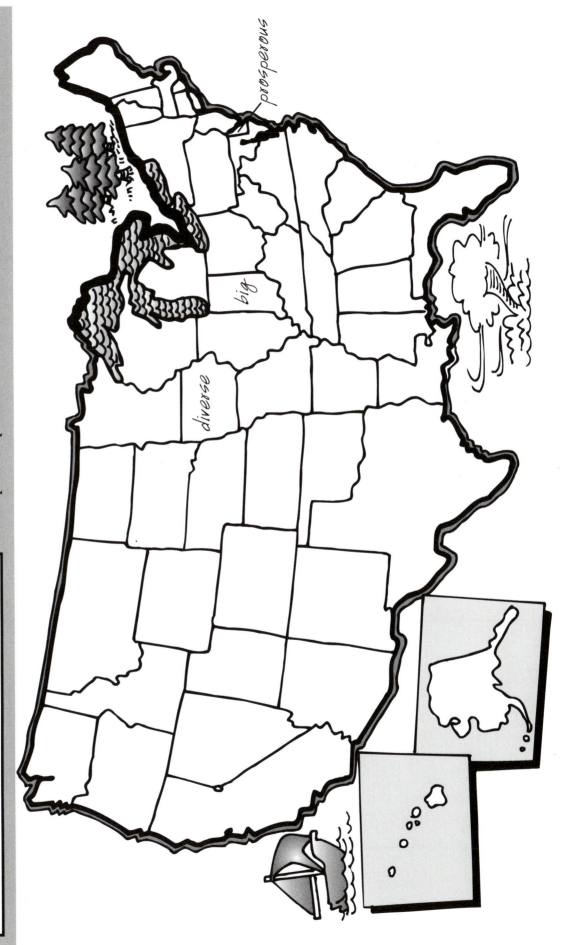

10

Spelling It Out

The letters U and N have been done for you.
Complete the wording for the rest of the letters
following the established pattern. When finished your work
should tell all who read it what the United States is all about.

U _nique_   union of people from all over the world

N _atural Resources_   water and forests and farmlands for all

I _____   _____

T _____   _____

E _____   _____

D _____   _____

S _____   _____

T _____   _____

A _____   _____

T _____   _____

E _____   _____

S _____   _____

Photo Sense

Someone once said, "A picture is worth a thousand words." It is true a photo can relate much information to an observant viewer. Your assignment is to think about what photographs you would take of your community to send to someone your age in Zimbabwe.

Your first assignment is to take ten photographs in your community. These ten photos should show as much about daily life in your community as possible. List the ten photos you would take.

_____   _____
_____   _____
_____   _____
_____   _____
_____   _____

Your second assignment is a little more difficult. It will require a little more thinking and will require you to be more selective. There are probably one hundred photographs that could be sent, but you can send only ten. The ten photographs should show Nmbaki in Zimbabwe what life in the state where you live is like. List the ten photos you will send.

_____   _____
_____   _____
_____   _____
_____   _____
_____   _____

Your final assignment as a photographer is a tough one. Once again you are limited to just ten photographs. This time your photos must accurately and comprehensively try to show Nmbaki what the United States is like. List the ten photos you will send.

_____   _____
_____   _____
_____   _____
_____   _____
_____   _____

Two! Four! Six! Eight! Who Should We Eliminate?

Some Facts:

☆ Rhode Island has only 1,540 square miles, making it our smallest state.

☆ Fewer people live in Wyoming (only 453,000) than in any other state.

☆ Hawaii is so far away. You have to fly there or take a boat.

☆ Most of Alaska is a frozen, mountainous area that can barely support anything.

☆ Florida is hot, sultry, swampy land.

☆ Something bad is happening all the time in New York City.

☆ More crimes happen in Louisiana than in any other state.

☆ California has earthquakes, mudslides, fires, a shortage of water and various disasters.

Think of it. Some states are not as valuable to the United States as others. Believe it or not a new law has been passed. We must get rid of (eliminate) one state.

What state do you think it should be? _____

What are the reasons we should eliminate this state? _____
_____
_____

OK, we were just joking. Let's think some more. What are the characteristics of a good state?
_____
_____

List several states that are lucky enough to be able to contribute quite significantly to our nation.
_____
_____

Each of our fifty states, and we really do want to keep them all, is unique. Which of our states do you feel is unique? _____
_____
_____

Why? _____
_____
_____

Living in Florisota or Florizona

Living in Florisota (half Florida and half Minnesota) might be really nice. In the summer months there would be the cool north woods and in the winter, when Minnesota is snow and ice, you could enjoy the balmy tropical breezes. But maybe you would rather live in New Kansas. This state would be half metropolitan and industrial and half gently rolling plains.

Put on your thinking cap. Manipulate the syllables of the names of our states and create some new names. California and Delaware could be called Caliware. Delasippi would be Delaware and Mississippi. Colohigan would be derived from Colorado and Michigan. Use the lines below to brainstorm and create some new state names.

_____

_____

_____

_____

Now, a change of the rules. Any new state name you create must include at least three syllables, each from the name of an existing state.

_____

_____

_____

_____

My five best new names are _____

_____

_____

Forcing Associations

Forcing Associations is taking two seemingly unrelated items and determining ways that they are similar. If you were asked how a fire engine is like an apple, you could reply by saying that on the outside most are red or that a fire engine has a hose to connect it to something and an apple has a stem to connect it to a tree. So pull on your thinking cap tightly and see what associations you can generate between the United States and each of the following.

How is the United States like a banana split? _____
_____
_____
_____

How is the United States like a hot air balloon? _____
_____
_____
_____

How is the United States like a raindrop? _____
_____
_____
_____

How is the United States like a feather? _____
_____
_____
_____

How is the United States like a roller coaster? _____
_____
_____
_____

Maps! Maps! Maps!

Name five different things you can find on a map of the United States.

_____

_____

_____

_____

Name five different things you can find on a road map.

_____

_____

_____

_____

Name five things you can find on a road map that you can't find on a map of the United States.

_____

_____

_____

_____

Which sell better, world maps or road maps? Why? _____

_____

_____

Why do maps need to be revised every few years? Can you list several reasons?

_____

_____

_____

_____

On the back, draw a map to show the way from your home to your school.

Bismarck or Pierre?

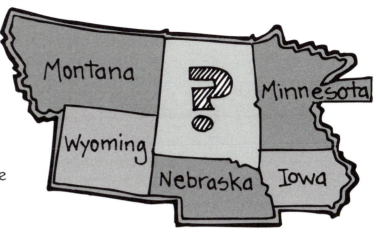

Does the map to the right look a little strange? Is a line missing? What is the name of the unlisted area?

The citizens of North Dakota and South Dakota voted and decided to become one state. The first thing they must do is come up with a new name. Do you have any ideas?

_____

Why do you think these people voted to become one state? List several reasons.

_____

_____

_____

_____

_____

Should the capital of this new state be Bismarck or Pierre or some other community? What are the positive and negative aspects of using one of the existing capital cities? Why would it be best to have a new capital city? Why would it be foolish to use Pierre or Bismarck? _____

_____

_____

_____

What are some other complications created by this merger? _____

_____

_____

How do you think the people of Minnesota or Montana feel?_____

_____

_____

Play around with the idea of merging the names of our states. Would you call Illinois and Indiana, Illiana or Indinois or something else? On the back side of this sheet, list some of your new creations.

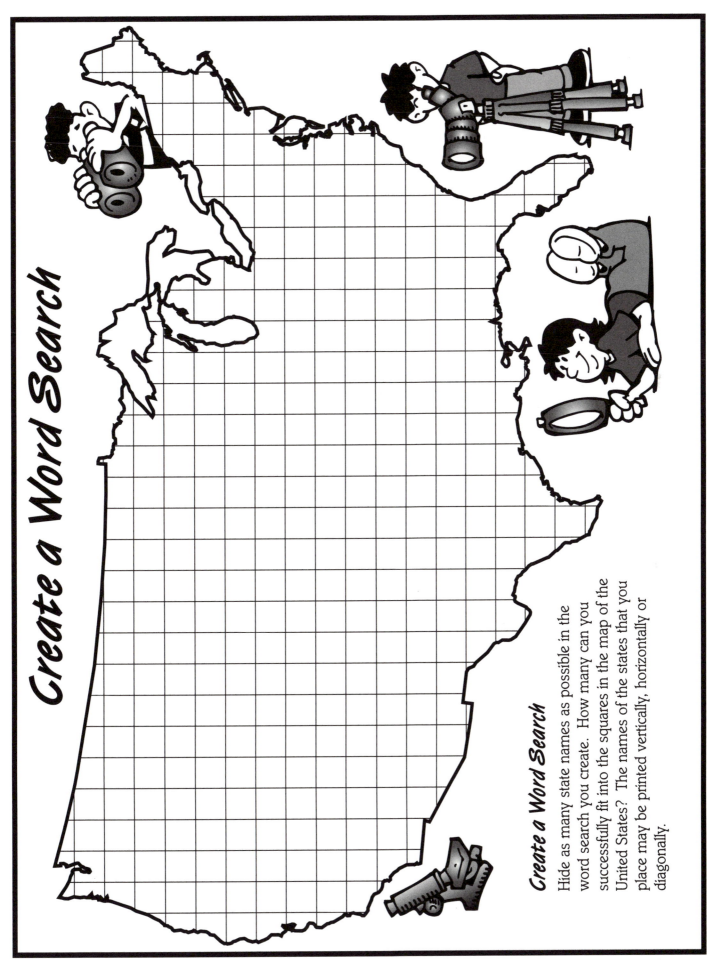

Create a Word Search

Create a Word Search

Hide as many state names as possible in the word search you create. How many can you successfully fit into the squares in the map of the United States? The names of the states that you place may be printed vertically, horizontally or diagonally.

What State Do You Think of . . . ?

What state do you think of when you think of . . . ?

mountains_____	good weather_____
cheese/Packers_____	peaches/peanuts_____
gambling_____	pineapples/surfing_____
vacations_____	Abraham Lincoln_____
10,000 lakes_____	automobiles/Motown sound_____
oranges_____	few faces/wide open spaces_____
country music_____	corn/hogs_____
movie stars_____	potatoes_____
bluegrass/horse races_____	great football teams_____
deserts/retirees_____	cranberries/capes_____
bears/ice_____	oil/cattle_____
cotton_____	skyscrapers_____

Now it is your turn to try to think of some additional word/state associations. If four of five people you ask respond with the same state as an answer, you have a winner. Sorry, you cannot list the names of cities or specific places. You could list Walt Disney but not Disney World. You could list Mardi Gras but not New Orleans.

_____   _____
_____   _____
_____   _____
_____   *hulas and leis/Hawaii*
Mardi Gras/Louisiana   _____
_____   _____
_____
_____
_____
_____
_____

Will It Fit in Texas?

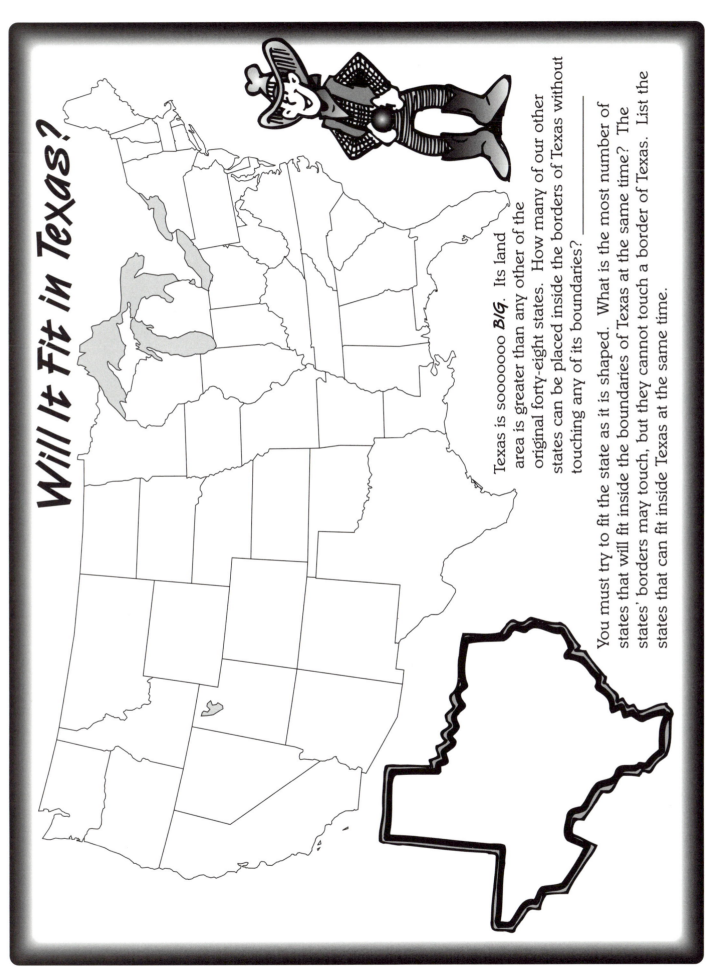

Texas is soooooo *Big*. Its land area is greater than any other of the original forty-eight states. How many of our other states can be placed inside the borders of Texas without touching any of its boundaries? _____

You must try to fit the state as it is shaped. What is the most number of states that will fit inside the boundaries of Texas at the same time? The states' borders may touch, but they cannot touch a border of Texas at the same time. List the states that can fit inside Texas at the same time.

Create a Symbol Map

You probably know more about the United States than you realize. As you work this exercise, you will discover what you know and what you don't know. But you will put only symbols on this map. Not one word, not one letter of the alphabet will be used. Just use symbols like letters. Place them wherever they should go.

Now it's your turn to create some more.

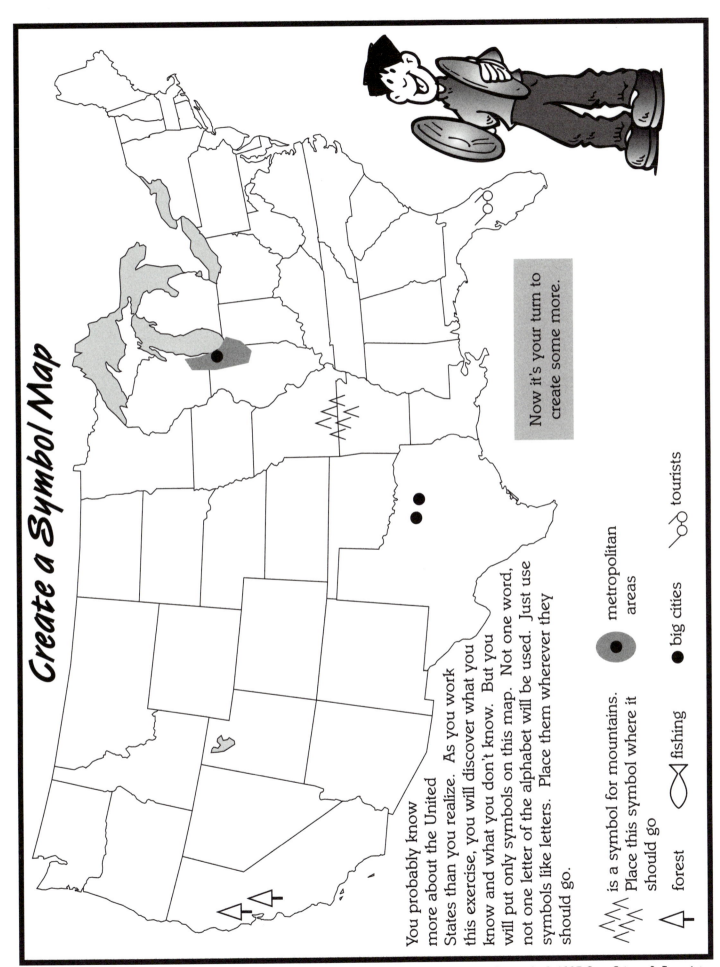

∧∧∧ is a symbol for mountains. Place this symbol where it should go

⟨ forest

⟨ fishing

⬭ metropolitan areas

● big cities

∞ tourists

Can You Get to Florida?

Work your way through the maze and see if you can arrive in Florida.

List some reasons why people go to Florida. _____

_____

_____

List some reasons why some people want to leave Florida. _____

_____

_____

On another sheet of paper create a maze to reach the state where you live. Make a list of reasons why someone should visit your state.

More for Mount Rushmore

Gustzon Borglum began his gigantic sculpture on Mount Rushmore in 1927. He worked on his creation for over fourteen years until his death in 1941. His tribute to Thomas Jefferson, Theodore Roosevelt, George Washington, and Abraham Lincoln was completed by his son Lincoln.

You have been asked to serve on a committee. Its purpose is to choose the people to be honored as the work of Mr. Borglum is continued by the finest sculptors of today.

Make a list of additional famous Americans whose faces should be added to Mount Rushmore. List ten possibilities and tell why each person should be considered.

1. _____ _____
2. _____ _____
3. _____ _____
4. _____ _____
5. _____ _____
6. _____ _____
7. _____ _____
8. _____ _____
9. _____ _____
10. _____ _____

Take a poll. Ask twenty-five neighbors, family members, people on the street who should be the next person to be enshrined on Mount Rushmore. Show each person your list of candidates. Do not allow anyone to see who others have voted for.

_____ is the winner of my poll.

Transportation

1. Besides people, what needs to be transported? _____

_____

_____

_____

2. Make a list of modes of transportation. _____

_____

_____

_____

3. What are the five most common modes of transportation used in the United States? Your number 1 should be the most common.

    (1) _____

    (2) _____

    (3) _____

    (4) _____

    (5) _____

4. List four modes of transportation that are not common any more. Tell why each is no longer common and what has replaced it.

_____

_____

_____

_____

5. We are constantly improving the ways we travel and the ways we move and send things. List some means of transportation that did not exist fifty years ago.

_____

_____

_____

6. What does the future hold in store for us? How will we be transporting people, messages, and cargo fifty years from now?

_____

_____

_____

Create a Billboard

The government of the United States has decided to place a billboard on the moon just in case someone from another world also lands there. The purpose of the billboard is to advertise the United States to encourage these space creatures to come and visit. What should that billboard say?

HOORAY for HOMETOWN U.S.A.

There are many neat and nifty things for a visitor to do in your hometown or city. Many of them could be enjoyed by taking a walk or bicycle ride. The Chamber of Commerce of your community has asked you to help plan a brochure (information sheet) about your hometown that includes places or things for tourists to enjoy.

Three buildings and two stores that a person from out of state or from Europe might enjoy are:	A restaurant or bakery or other place to grab a snack, goodies or nice meal would include:

Senior citizens might especially enjoy spending an hour or so doing the following:

_____   _____

_____   _____

If you were creating a photo album, what photos of your community would you include?	What recreational activities are available for tourists who come to your community?

Four things children might like to do when they are in my community are:

_____   _____

_____   _____

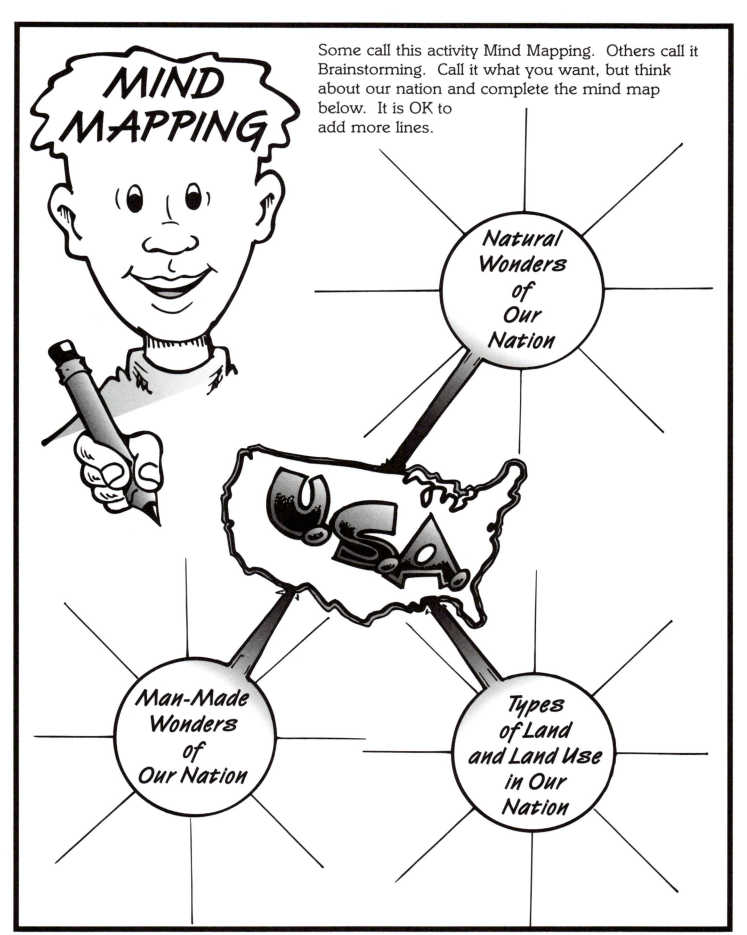

Some call this activity Mind Mapping. Others call it Brainstorming. Call it what you want, but think about our nation and complete the mind map below. It is OK to add more lines.

MIND MAPPING

Natural Wonders of Our Nation

U.S.A.

Man-Made Wonders of Our Nation

Types of Land and Land Use in Our Nation

TAKE A WALKABOUT!

There are many neat things to do in your town or city. So, put on some comfortable shoes and take a walkabout.

I live in _____, _____, _____

Approximately _____ people live in the same community as I do.

I found the following quiet, almost empty places.

_____
_____
_____
_____
_____
_____
_____

What jobs do you see the people of your community performing?

_____
_____
_____
_____
_____
_____
_____
_____
_____

I discovered the following busy, bustling places:

_____
_____
_____
_____
_____
_____
_____
_____
_____
_____

Places where I would like to spend more time . . .

_____
_____
_____
_____
_____
_____
_____
_____
_____

Create a Quilt Block

WANTED:

Quilt block designers. Create a quilt block design for your town, city, or state (or one you would like to visit). Using colored pens or pencils, sketch the design you created in the space below.

Quilts are meant to be beautiful and, sometimes, to tell a story as well as to be used for warmth.

Still others were made from scraps of old clothing and were

A famous quilt is the one recently designed in memory of the people who died of AIDS.

Other quilts show pictures of events that were important in the lives of the family who owned them.

A Plot! A Plan! A Plat!

The dictionary says that a plat is a small plot of ground. It is also a plan of a piece of land with actual or proposed features. In the designated space below draw a plat of your neighborhood, your farm or the block where you live. Be sure to draw all that you can remember being there.

Now that you have completed the above, select one building and draw its layout (blueprint). You might not be quite sure just what goes where, but do the best you can.

Later, when you have a chance, check out what you drew. See how closely you came to the real thing.

My Mind Is a Camera. I Can Take a Picture of Anything I Want to Remember

Picture the following without looking around.

1. How many desks are in your classroom?

2. How many chairs are in your living room?

3. Name three items (pictures) on the bulletin board.

4. How many windows in your house or apartment?

5. How many cabinets (filing/storage) in your classroom?

6. What is your teacher wearing today?

7. Name three items on your mother's kitchen counter.

8. How many pairs of shoes are in your closet and bedroom?

Another Kodak moment awaits you. Draw a picture of your room as it is right now. If you don't have a room of your own, that's okay. Use the one you share or choose another room in your house.

Vacation Time

A list of "stuff" I want to pack to put in the car for the cross-country trip.

_____
_____
_____
_____
_____
_____
_____
_____
_____
_____
_____
_____
_____
_____
_____
_____
_____
_____
_____
_____
_____
_____
_____
_____
_____

Your parents have just informed you and your sister (a year younger) and your brother (two years younger) that the family is taking a vacation this summer. This vacation includes a car trip across the country from New York to Los Angeles.

You will be responsible for keeping yourself and your siblings amused during the long, six-day car trip. After some thought, you decide to base the activities on what you see as you pass through the various states and cities.

List below some of the possible things you will do to pass the many hours in the car.

Car Fun Activities

1. _____
_____

2. _____
_____

3. _____
_____

4. _____
_____

5. _____
_____

6. _____
_____

7. _____
_____

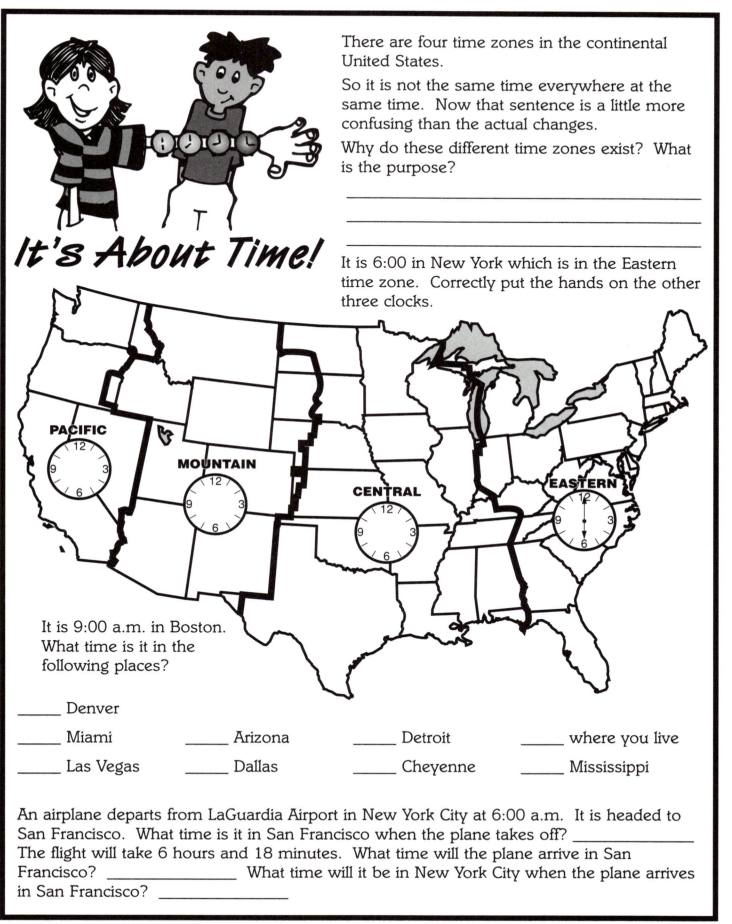

It's About Time!

There are four time zones in the continental United States.

So it is not the same time everywhere at the same time. Now that sentence is a little more confusing than the actual changes.

Why do these different time zones exist? What is the purpose?

_____

_____

_____

It is 6:00 in New York which is in the Eastern time zone. Correctly put the hands on the other three clocks.

PACIFIC

MOUNTAIN

CENTRAL

EASTERN

It is 9:00 a.m. in Boston. What time is it in the following places?

_____ Denver

_____ Miami   _____ Arizona   _____ Detroit   _____ where you live

_____ Las Vegas   _____ Dallas   _____ Cheyenne   _____ Mississippi

An airplane departs from LaGuardia Airport in New York City at 6:00 a.m. It is headed to San Francisco. What time is it in San Francisco when the plane takes off? _____
The flight will take 6 hours and 18 minutes. What time will the plane arrive in San Francisco? _____ What time will it be in New York City when the plane arrives in San Francisco? _____

Plot-a-Plate

Create a license plate for your state or a state you would like to visit. It should have a slogan, artwork, a color scheme, and, of course, the obligatory numbers and letters. It could be a vanity plate.

Clothes R Us

It is December 20th. People are out and about doing what they normally do on a typical December 20th. Some are on vacation. Others are doing a little last minute Christmas shopping. Most are at work. But what clothing are they wearing, not just in the office but outside on the way to the office?

List inside the outline of each state what locals and visitors to that area would be wearing.

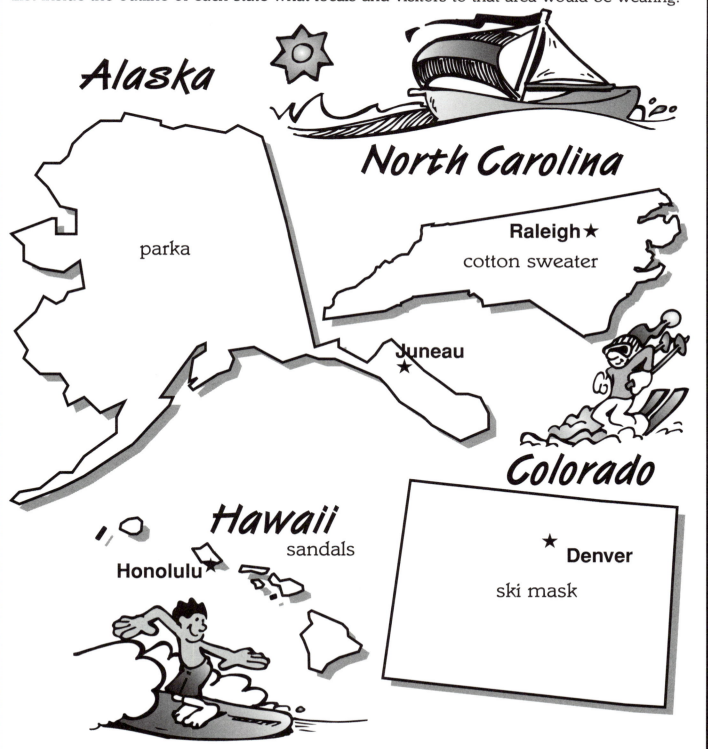

Alaska

parka

North Carolina

Raleigh ★
cotton sweater

Juneau ★

Colorado

★ Denver

ski mask

Hawaii

sandals

Honolulu

Map   Play

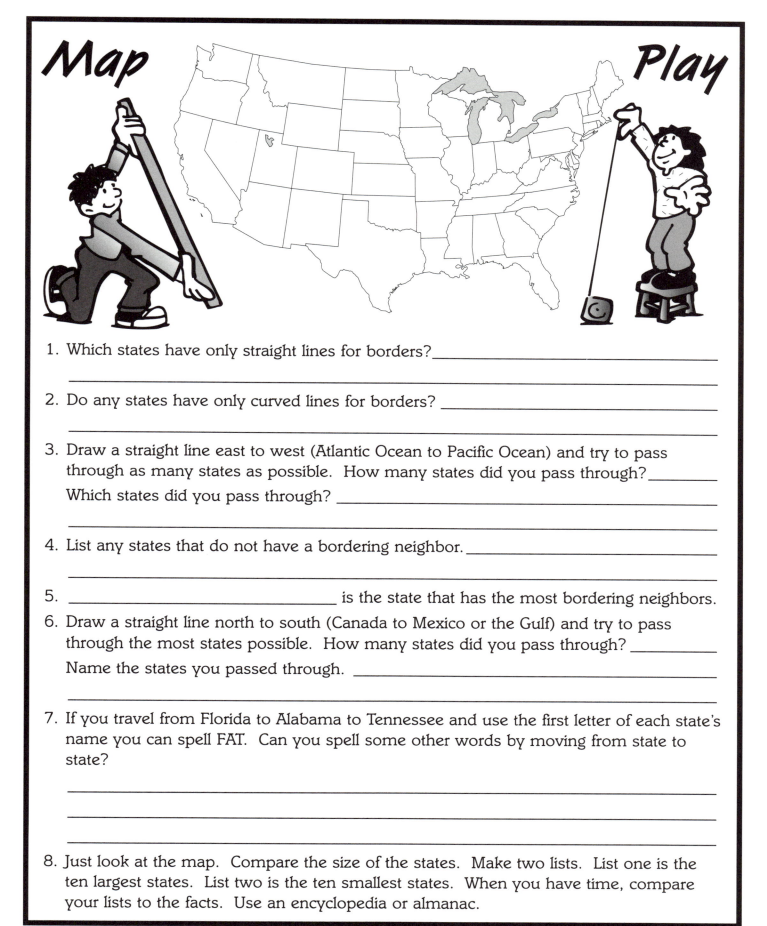

1. Which states have only straight lines for borders?_____
   _____

2. Do any states have only curved lines for borders? _____
   _____

3. Draw a straight line east to west (Atlantic Ocean to Pacific Ocean) and try to pass
   through as many states as possible. How many states did you pass through?_____
   Which states did you pass through? _____
   _____

4. List any states that do not have a bordering neighbor._____
   _____

5. _____ is the state that has the most bordering neighbors.

6. Draw a straight line north to south (Canada to Mexico or the Gulf) and try to pass
   through the most states possible. How many states did you pass through? _____
   Name the states you passed through. _____
   _____

7. If you travel from Florida to Alabama to Tennessee and use the first letter of each state's
   name you can spell FAT. Can you spell some other words by moving from state to
   state?

   _____
   _____
   _____

8. Just look at the map. Compare the size of the states. Make two lists. List one is the
   ten largest states. List two is the ten smallest states. When you have time, compare
   your lists to the facts. Use an encyclopedia or almanac.

Too-Big Texas

That's right! Texas is just too big. All the other states except Alaska are jealous. Delaware and Rhode Island just feel so small.

Are there any good reasons to make Texas more than one state?_____
_____
_____

Does anything exist that would help decision makers decide where to divide Texas?
_____
_____

Inside the map of Texas write and draw what you know. Can you name the neighbors of Texas? What are the large cities? Where are they located? Can you make some symbols to show the mountains, forests, products of Texas?

What would be a good name for the new states? No, you cannot use north, south, east or west.

_____

_____

_____

When you have time, get some reference materials and learn more about Texas. How far is it north to south, east to west? How long would it take to drive from Oklahoma to Mexico? What does Texas contribute to the United States? What is the land and climate of Texas like? Where would you like to go in Texas?

No Longer United

Things change, even nations. For many years Germany was East and West. Now it is one nation. Czechoslovakia is now the Czech Republic and Slovakia, two independent nations. The Soviet Union no longer exists. Who knows how many nations Yugoslavia will become. Some French Canadians want to be an independent French speaking nation. It could happen to the United States. What if it did?

The above map shows the division the leaders agreed upon. What had to be done to create two nations? What additional things must be done? What complications will arise? What will the two names be? What cities will be the capitals? How will the two nations differ? In which one would you want to live? Why? Which will be the stronger nation? What will the East need to buy from the West? What will the West need to buy from the East? Who will own the Mississippi River? On the reverse side write some of your questions and thoughts.

Think about our fifty states. What makes a state great? Think about climate, size, population, shape, and location. Think about towns, villages, cities, industry, parks, and farmland. Don't forget to think about topography (the lay of the land), vegetation, and natural resources. Think, think, and think and then in the space below create the ideal state . . . Utopia. Draw a map of this ideal state. Use words and symbols to indicate what it is like.

Scrambled Capitals

First unscramble the letters and spell the names of ten of our capital cities. Then name the correct state for each capital.

Second, do your own scrambling. Choose any other ten states and scramble the letters for each capital city. See if a friend or family member can unscramble your efforts.

Finally on the back, list any other capital cities that you can.

	CAPITAL	STATE
NOTABROGUE	_____	_____
SUNATI	_____	_____
CROKTILLET	_____	_____
LIPSINGFRED	_____	_____
DAMISNO	_____	_____
MIACLUBO	_____	_____
SUMCLUBO	_____	_____
THECLANORS	_____	_____
NANALIPSO	_____	_____

My Scrambled Capitals

1. _____
2. _____
3. _____
4. _____
5. _____

6. _____
7. _____
8. _____
9. _____
10. _____